Best Developer Job Ever!

5-step plan to dream jobs, high salaries & career freedom

TABLE OF CONTENTS

It's time to move on 7
    But first 8

5 Steps for Moving to a Great Job 11
    Get Clarity on your Strengths 11
    Define your Objectives 11
    Expand your Network 12
    Promote Yourself 12
    Get Quality Interviews 13

Get Clarity on your Strengths 15
    Understand your strengths 15
    Make a list of skills you have and are good at 18
    Brainstorm about positions for which your skills are useful 19
    Brainstorm how to meet people already in that position 21
    Brainstorm how you can help people in the above places 22
    Get Clarity on your Strengths. You deserve this 23

Define your Objectives 27
    Write about what you want financially 27
    Write about what you want personally 28
    Write about what you want professionally 29
    Go back and fill in more details 29
    Use the SMART template to better define your goals 30
    Define your Objectives. In a SMART way! 32

Expand your Network 35

    Join Facebook and LinkedIn groups related to your desired position 37

    Join mailing lists of open source projects related to your position 37

    Using Twitter, follow 30 or more influential people 38

    Find meetups in your area and attend in person meetings 38

    Go where your prospects are. Online and offline 38

    Listen. And look for ways to help others 39

    Spend time helping others – the 5 minute rule 40

    Expand your Network. Expand your help 41

Promote Yourself 44

    First: understand it is not about you! 45

    Improve your social media profiles; make them more professional 45

    Write small articles about the skills you are good at 47

    Write about your experience with open source software 48

    Answer questions from members in your groups 48

    Share what you ALREADY know and what you are good at 49

    Post articles to Medium.com 49

    Post articles to LinkedIn 50

    Do presentations 50

    At local meetups 51

    On YouTube 52

    At local companies 53

    Work on a company's open source project 55

    Promote Yourself. The right way 56

Get Quality Interviews 59

- Get interviews in all those places 61
- Offer free consultations about your best skills 61
- Offer to do a project for them 63
- Get Quality Interviews. To be hired, not rejected 64

Next steps… 70

Moving because I DO have a Choice 73

Moving because I DON'T have a Choice 78

References 81

It's time to move on

There are times you feel like changing jobs for something better. We have all been there. Moving to another job isn't easy. And it is an extremely important decision.

Taking another job means leaving the familiarity of what you do now and stepping into the unknown. Your motivation for changing jobs might be for a better salary, or more interesting and challenging work. Maybe it's not motivation… You didn't have a choice.

Whatever your reasons are, you are making the change to have something better, and that's the goal.

This could be because you don't like your job right now, or because you outgrew your company. You might feel your current job is not challenging enough for you to reach your full potential. You might not be learning anymore, improving your skills or learning new technologies.

Those are good reasons, but there are many more reasons for changing jobs.

You may not have a choice. You were fired, or your company went bankrupt or had other challenges that affected the bottom line. You've decided to move to another city or even another country. Those could be some stressful or even scary situations.

Moving to another job doesn't mean moving to a different company. It could be moving to a new position or a promotion or changing to another department where you will work on different types of projects.

But how do you actually move to another job or another position? How do you move to another city or another country? How do you get a new job when everything else has failed and you lost your job?

That's a serious matter. And there are very good ways of doing this, and this is what this book is about.

But first...

My name is Bruno Souza, and I'm worldwide known as the Brazilian JavaMan.

That's how most people know me. I'm a Java developer since 1995, and I've been part of a lot of amazing Java projects. Millions of people use code that I wrote, and I did a lot of cool stuff in software development. I'm a Java Champion and served on the board of the Open Source Initiative, the Java Community Process and other organizations. I also built companies and products. Some of them even had some success! I'm also a puppeteer and known as "the Guy with the Flag", but that's another story.

But... What is less well known, is that for more than 20 years, I've been helping developers to get hired for amazing projects, to work in fantastic teams.

You see... When I was at university, I was visiting my parents. The day started perfect, a good family day, with lively conversations. It soon turned into a big disagreement between me and my father, about my career decisions.

Disagreement is an understatement... We had a big, ugly fight...

To this day, I'm not proud of it...

In the middle of this, the phone rang. The voice on the other side told me about an opportunity at Sun Microsystems. It was my friend Luiz, who referred me to his friends at Sun.

At that moment, my dad still mad and against my decision, sat down on his computer, and helped me write my first resume. With his help, I got the job at Sun. One week later, John Gage did Java's first public demonstration. One thing led to another, and here I am, 20-something years later, the Brazilian JavaMan.

With his example, my dad showed that helping me grow my career, help me follow my own path, was more important than convincing me to do what he thought was best.

From that day on, my focus was clear. No matter what I did -- whether it was Java development, sharing as an evangelist, building a consulting business, working on open source, managing communities -- my biggest goal has been to help developers grow their careers. Help developers follow their own path.

During those 20+ years, I have helped thousands of developers to improve their skills, learn new technologies, be up-to date with the market. I've helped developers to work on the best projects and most amazing teams, by sharing what they know.

Following my dad's example, I've helped developers move from small companies to big ones. And from big to small ones. Change careers. Get their first job. Move from bad to great projects in the same company. Many turned lame projects into amazing ones without having to move. With the right support, developers got promoted, increased their salaries, and got new jobs after being fired. I even helped devs launch products and create companies.

Whatever path you plan to follow in your developer career, count on me to help you achieve what you want. In this book I've put my best suggestions to help you move. No matter what moving means to you.

Don't wait. Become your best version. Let's jump right in!

5 Steps for Moving to a Great Job

There are five steps you can take to get yourself into another job.

But not just any job. A great job is one that will help you grow. That matches who you are and what you want to do in the future. That respects you for what you know.

Get Clarity on your Strengths

It's very, very important that you get clarity on your strengths and your focus. You must fully realize what you are very good at.

It's difficult to move to another job if you don't know what you have to offer. You can actually move to another job that requires more qualifications than you have, but you have to understand what strengths you can bring to the new position. The things you are good at will play an important role in your next job.

That's your first step.

Define your Objectives

The second step is to define your objectives.

If you don't understand what you want - what you want for your life, for your career, what you want professionally, personally, financially - then you might move to a position that's of less value to you in relation to your objectives than the one you have now.

A lot of times people move away from positions they dislike for some reason and move into even worse positions. It's very important that you understand what your objectives are, and get clarity on them.

Once you know what you want, and you decide it's time to move on, you can do so. It's better to get this clear soon. Otherwise you might be forced to move on, and without defining your objectives, your options become limited.

Expand your Network

After defining your objectives and deciding to move on, you have to analyze your network.

The best way to get a job is by reaching out to your network. Research shows that you only have a 1.2% chance of getting a job through an online application. At the same time, 30% of the hires happen from a referral by another employee. A recruiter told me that it's 45 times more likely that you get a new job by someone referring you to a company than if you are not referred.

Your network is extremely valuable. So are the people you know. They're your friends. It is important to improve your network of business acquaintances and friends, to make it stronger, and expand it in size while you're looking for another position.

Promote Yourself

Once your network is as strong as you can make it and you've increased it in size as much as you can.... then what? The next step is to promote yourself.

But you must do it in the right way. If you promote yourself the wrong way, your network will consider you annoying and pushy. If you promote yourself in a desperate way, they will feel sorry for you, and that won't land you a job.

If you promote yourself the right way, people are going to know what you want, they are going to know what strengths you can bring to a position, and they will suggest you to their companies, to their projects, to their teams.

Promoting yourself the right way is a decisive point.

Get Quality Interviews

The fifth step is obtaining quality interviews.

This is key. Through your network, because you're promoting yourself, you can get amazingly high-quality interviews; sometimes for jobs that don't even exist yet. Out of 9 people that get an internal referral, 1 get a job.

Conversely, if you just get interviews by sending your resume to a company, you're limiting yourself to a very narrow and small subset of possibilities. From external processes, like sending your resume online, out of 33, 1 get a job.

If you get quality interviews, you will be on your way to getting a great job. Lots of people are getting amazing results doing this.

These are 5 steps that work and will make a difference in your job search. Let's take a closer look and see exactly what you need to do in each one of them.

Get Clarity on your Strengths

As a first step, you must have clarity on your strengths and a solid understanding of the things you're very good at.

Understanding your skill set is vital. Once you are clear what your skills are and you've determined what you like to do, you can prove to others what it is that you do well. You become a master at expressing your worth.

You are skillful at many more things than you might imagine. Everything you've ever done, all the things you've accomplished in your life required certain skills. But, in looking at all the skills you possess right now, which ones matter? Which ones will make a difference in your new position? Which ones can have an impact on the company itself?

Once you are clear about what you have to bring to a certain type of position and how you can impact a specific company, it will be much easier for you to find the right position. One that you will love going to each day because you know you are very good at what you do.

Once you have clarity about what you can bring to the table, it's a lot easier for you to get other people to see the value you have to offer a company. So instead of looking for any kind of job and applying for any position that you find, go after the BEST positions, the ones that are an excellent match for your skill set.

How do you get this clarity? That's a little bit of work. It might take you a few minutes, a couple of hours or even days. But don't stop until you gain clarity on your strengths. Taking this action step seriously is crucially important when you are changing jobs.

Understand your strengths

Ask yourself questions to understand what your strengths are.

What do you enjoy doing in your free time? You do things in your free time because you want to, because you like doing it, and because you are good at it. So what do you like to do in your free time?

Whatever it is you enjoy doing involves implementing skills. Whether you like dancing, drawing, playing board games or getting involved in sports, there are skills involved in doing them. What are they? Think about each moment you are engaged with doing the thing you love and you'll begin to see the skills you use to actually accomplish what you enjoy doing.

There's all kinds of different skills: communication skills, skill in different physical movements from professional athleticism to recreational sports, team and collaboration skills. Playing soccer, for example, involves collaboration; it is a team effort. And that same ability to work on a team can apply to software development or other projects. Understand what strengths you bring to the things you like to do in your free time.

It's important to understand the skills you engage in your free time, because you do these things even though nobody is paying you. Actually, you usually SPEND money to do the things you love. Some people learn new technologies so they can have fun, like online gaming. Some people learn new skills to enhance sporting activities, like taking golf lessons to improve their game. Find out what you love to do and how you go about doing it or becoming better at it, because these things are important attributes you bring to a job.

Then consider the job you have now. What do you love about it? Do you like to program? Do you like to discuss things with people? Do you like to make decisions? Do you like the communication aspect of it? Do you like to talk with customers? What parts of your current job do you like?

The things you enjoy about your current job are most likely things you are good at. Most people think they like something and then they become good at it, but the real truth is that you're good at something first, and because you're good at it you get results, and then you start liking those things.

Find the things you're good at, the things you like. Discover what you do that cause people around you to say, "Hey, great job! You did it right! Well done." Write those things down to make sure you understand your strengths.

What were you good at as a child? When you were a teenager? Write those things down too, because the things you are very good at from an early age are probably skills you've built upon for years; you've been improving those skills since then. You might be skilled at talking to people or solving problems. Or you enjoyed puzzles when you were a child and you still like them, but the puzzles you work on today aren't a game, they've become problems you must solve as part of your job or the day-to-day process of living.

Try to remember the things you liked to do when you were a child, and divide those things into skills. What are the things your family and friends think you are very good at? What things do you do that make them say, "Wow, you're good at this! You do this well." When you played sports, were you good in teamwork? When you played video games, was solving problems what attracted you? When you played instruments, was the organization of the band schedule your strength? Write those individual skills down. Understanding these skills will help you nail down what you're good at, where your strengths are.

Another way to look at this is to think of the people you admire. We usually admire people because we want to be like them. We admire their skills or the things they are able to do. Many times it's because we want to be able to do those things, too.

A lot of times, you already have some of those skills you admire. Other times, it is more a desire you can use to go in the right direction. Consider your skill set based on what you admire about someone else. You admire people who can go on stage and give an outstanding presentation. You can also learn to give a presentation. Or someone you admire is very good at writing difficult code. You can also become good at writing difficult code.

Who do you admire? Write it down. What do they do? Write it down. What is important to you? Write it down. Now you understand a little bit about your strengths, the things you are good at.

You just made an initial list of things you are good at. Keep that list in mind. We're going to work with it along the way.

Make a list of skills you have and are good at

Let me tell you about skills. Skills are different from knowledge. Knowledge involves things you know. If you read a book, you gain knowledge. Skills are things you do that you do well. You can't read a book about programming and then immediately become a good programmer. You have to do a lot of programming to become a good programmer.

That's true for a lot of things. You can't read a book about soccer and then become a great soccer player. Skills don't work like this. You can't read a book about cooking and then suddenly be a great cook. It doesn't work like this. You have to play soccer and cook often to be great at it. You have to do things to get the skills.

You can't read a book about negotiation and then be a great negotiator. You can't read a book about networking and suddenly be a great networker. Remember that you have to do things.

You can't just read this book about getting a new job or moving to a new job. If you don't do the things we're talking about here, it's not going to help. You have to acquire the skills.

Now look at all the things you said you like, the things that you enjoy doing in your free time, the things that you like to do at work, the things that you like to do since your childhood, the things that people tell you you're good at. Think of all these and list these skills, because these skills that you already have are what matters.

It's not about what you know, it's about what skills you already have. Knowing a programming language doesn't help if you don't have skill in solving problems with code.

List all the skills, all the things you actually do. Not the things you know, the things that you do. Those are going to be the basis for everything else you're going to find out about your strengths. It's not about specific products or technologies, it's about the things you do, and even skills that go beyond your job.

Don't simply list the skills related to your job. List the skills related to sports. List things you do in your free time. Things you do in your family life. Things you do daily. Maybe you're very good at organizing. You're very good at organizing the life of your family or organizing your house; that means you're very good at organizing things. You can apply these skills you are listing to your job.

Think about it for a few minutes and make a list of the important skills you have that you do every day, or frequently, or at work, or in your free time. All these skills you can carry into the workplace.

Brainstorm about positions for which your skills are useful

Now that you understand what skills you have, let's work a little bit on the position you want to get. What is the next step on the ladder of who you want to be?

You want to move on. You want to move on from your project to another project. You want to move on from your company to another company. You want to move on from your city to another city. You want to move, or you have to move. What's the next thing you want to do?

Let's brainstorm a little bit about which positions you want. Think about the position you'd like to have, then go to the Internet and search for what skills are needed in that position.

Maybe it's the skills of a project manager, a QA manager, or some type of creative manager, or of a scrum master. Or it's the skills of a senior developer, a Java developer or a developer of artificial intelligence.

The key word here is "skill".

To do this, go on the Internet and search for the position you're looking for, plus the word "skills".

Let's say you want to be a big data developer. Search for "skills of a big data developer". Do this several times for the different positions you are interested in.

Once you find two, three or four of those positions you're interested in, list the skills. Take a look at those lists of skills and compare them with the skills you already have.

As an example, if you want to be a software developer. A software developer has to have skills like solving problems, writing code, and reading code. Or let's say you want to be a senior developer. A senior developer would have communication and design skills.

Try to match those skills with the skills you already have. See which position would be the best ones for you. It's important that the positions you are looking for match the interest and skills you have now, and the things you want to have in the future.

When you want to move on, it's not about learning new things, applying new skills, and then moving on. It's about moving forward with what you already have. Take a look at what skills you have now and how you can use those skills to position yourself for the jobs you want.

Now that you know the skills you have, you can see that some of the positions are better than others. Keep brainstorming. Keep thinking about new positions and new situations. Talk with your friends, see what kinds of positions they suggest for you and try to match the skills you have with the skills necessary for those positions.

See which positions are the best match for you. Some positions might require skills you haven't yet mastered, but having some skills at basic levels is a good start. You can work on developing them later on. Right now, you're just trying to figure out what kind of position, what kind of great work you could do immediately.

Brainstorm how to meet people already in that position

The next step is to figure out where you can find people who already work in the position you are interested in.

Let's say you want to be a senior software developer, a senior Java developer, or you want to be a manager or a project manager. A big data project manager, for example. Let's figure out where you can find people that have those skills.

Start by searching for Meetups, Facebook groups, and LinkedIn groups that focus on that particular position.

On meetup.com look for Java meetups, senior developer meetups, or project manager meetups. Join those groups and go to the meetings.

Search Facebook for groups on any position you are interested in and join the groups. Get involved in the discussions.

Go to LinkedIn and search for groups that have people working in the positions you're interested in. Join those groups and reach out to the people in them.

If you want to be a CIO, search for groups that have people with CIO positions. You want to be a designer? Search for groups designers participate in. It doesn't matter which position you're looking for. Search for and join groups that have people in those positions. As a hint, most groups (but not all) will accept you even if you're not in that position yet.

Another thing you can do is search for open source projects related to the position you want.

Let's say, for example, you want to be an architect, a software architect. What kind of open source software are architects part of? If you're looking at open source projects that require or facilitate multiple integrations, an architect is probably going to be part of, or be using, those projects. Projects dealing with the cloud, microservices, IDEs, or design tools would probably have architects either working on the project or as part of the community.

You want to be around people who hold your desired position. Go find projects that are interesting for people in those positions and join them. Join mailing lists for open source projects. Join all the groups where people congregate who have the position you want.

Brainstorm how you can help people in the above places

Spend some time thinking about your skills. Is there something you can teach people in those groups?

You might be thinking, "Well, I don't know. I'm not a senior developer yet. How can I teach anything to senior developers?" I'm sure, if you have good communication skills, for example, senior developers need communication skills. So, if you have good communication skills, you could teach something about improving communication skills.

You may have to study a little bit so you can teach a little bit more, but if you already have good communication skills, you can do this. You can have good networking skills or good negotiation skills, or you know a lot about Java development and you could teach a little bit of Java development to architects or senior developers who don't know Java.

What is one thing you already know that you could help those people with? What is it they're looking for? Don't think about you. Think about them. What are they looking for? They want to improve their careers, too. The same as you. What could you help them with? You have some time and you could help them with their projects. I'm sure that if you think a little, you'll figure out how you could help some of them with something.

Also, brainstorm other little things you could do to help. You could help organize events. Or help by explaining some kind of technology. Maybe you're a great runner, and you could help architects or senior developers that want to learn how to run. Or you are very fit and you could help architects or senior developers become fit. There's all kinds of things you can offer to help them with that don't need to be directly related to the things you want to be.

Everyone needs to learn something. Remember, it's all about offering what you already know.

What things could you teach? What things could you help others with? It could be just a small group of people. Not every architect wants to run, but those that do would love to have someone that is a good runner to help them.

Later on in the book we're going to discuss how you can use this knowledge to actually create or expand your network. Right now, you need to think about it. It's important right now that you brainstorm things that you already know that could help other people who are already in the position you want to be in.

Get Clarity on your Strengths. You deserve this

You now have a clear vision of your strengths because you listed all the skills you have. You already matched your skills with the ones needed in the position that you want to be working in. Now you know which skills you already have that would match which kind of position, so when you go to an interview you have something to say because you know what that position needs.

You also know where to find people that are already working in this position. If you go to Meetups, Facebook groups, and LinkedIn groups, you can actually ask people there. What kind of skills do I need? How do I improve on these skills? I'm very good at coding, but I need better communication skills. How did you acquire your communication skills? You can start learning from them what it took to get into those positions.

Finally, you are brainstorming things you can do to help them improve their careers. Now you understand that you have information and skills that can be useful to them.

Then what happens?

Having clarity about your strengths, it's a lot easier for you to talk with people. It's a lot easier for you to promote yourself. It's a lot easier for you to grow your network. It's a lot easier for you to define your objective because you know what skills you have. You also know the skills you are lacking. Once you look at the positions, you know the skills you have and the skills you don't have.

It's also a lot easier for you to go after the skills you don't have yet. Amazingly, it's even possible to get a position working for a particular company that requires skills you don't have. You can say, "I want to work for you, and I'm going after the skills I'm missing."

A lot of times you're going to find out there is not a big difference between what you have and what you need to have. Frequently we get this idea that we don't have what it takes. But if you understand your strengths, it can become clear that you do have most of what is needed, and then you can go after the missing pieces.

I have a friend, Rafael, and I helped him find his strengths. He looked at everything he did. He looked at the things he likes to do. He looked at things he knew how to do well, and he found that he loved best practices for software development. He found the things he was good at with best practices. Rafael got clarity in his strengths, and from that point he went on to create, in a very short time, a project and a book about reducing bugs and stress in a project. He started getting dozens of job offers just because he talked about his strength.

So finding your strength, understanding your strength, is extremely important to prepare for the things you want to do.

Define your Objectives

One of the biggest problems people have when they're trying to move to another job, another position or another company, is the lack of clear objectives. Having clear objectives helps you understand where you're going and lets you know when you've arrived there.

When you're traveling, for example, you know which city you're going to and you will know when you arrive there. You might not know the exact route, but knowing where you want to get, you can figure out the path, and know whether or not you're getting closer to the destination. That is a good objective.

When you are clear about the place you want to get to you can measure both your progress and whether or not you ever get there. I talk with many developers about objectives. Many have objectives so generic that often they have already achieved them and don't even realize it. They don't see they are already there. So they keep investing time, effort and even money trying to get to a place they are already at…

Having good objectives is important, because once you understand where you want to go, it's possible, and a lot easier, to create a path to get there. You might not know how to get to the objective, but once you decide what it is you want, you can look around and find the ways and means to get there.

How do you create good objectives, then?

Write about what you want financially

First of all, let's do a little exercise so you can start creating new objectives right now. On a blank piece of paper, write your financial objectives. How much do you want to earn? How much do you need to earn?

What do you want to do that requires money? Do you want to buy a house? Do you want to go on a trip? Take your family to Disney World or go on a trip by yourself?

Once you know what is it you want to do that requires money, get clarity on how much money you will need to meet the objective.

Exactly how much money does that thing require? When do you want it? A year from now? Five years? Ten months from now? If you're going to buy a house; it's a long-term project. It can take you more time.

Understand what is it you want financially. Based on that, how much money do you need to make? How much money do you want to make? What kind of salary would you like to earn? Write those things down.

Now that you understand what you want financially, let's move to your personal goals.

Write about what you want personally

On a piece of paper, write your personal goals.

What are the things you want to do personally? Do you want to learn a new language, for example? Do you want to visit far-off places? Do you want to help your family somehow? Or maybe you want to help your parents or some friends that need help. You may want to help your church.

What are your personal objectives? What are the things you want to do personally? Maybe you want to do crazy things like parachute out of an airplane or climb a mountain. Or you want to lose weight. All these examples are personal objectives. Make sure you get clear on them.

Now take a look at the things you wrote down and provide more details about each of them. Write down when you want them to happen. Next year, next month, in the next six months? Put some deadlines on the things you want to do.

Write about what you want professionally

Now that you have some idea of your financial and personal objectives, let's discuss your professional objectives. What do you want to do professionally?

Do you want to get a raise? Do you want to earn a larger salary? Do you want to learn new technologies? Do you want to work on specific projects? Do you want to impact the world somehow? Do you want to eventually create a startup and have your own company? Do you want to grow in the company you work for and become a director or CEO or CTO? What do you want professionally?

Put it all down on paper.

A quick tip: this is about you. You don't need to think about what other people want you to want. It's not about them. It's about you. Don't be afraid to put down all the things you want. A lot of times when we write down objectives we're thinking, "Well, what my family will think?" Or, "What are my friends going to think?" Or we think that people don't move successfully from one industry to another. They don't have the courage to move even though they want to completely change their careers. But they don't make a change because they keep thinking about what other people are going to think. Remember, these objectives are not about what others will think. They are about you.

Think about what you want. Go back to your notes and take a look at your skills. Decide what skills you have that you could put to good use right now towards your objectives. How are your objectives related to your skills?

Now you have a better understanding of what you want to do professionally.

Go back and fill in more details

This step is very important. Unclear objectives are bad and unhelpful. You should have something like 10 to 15 goals that you wrote for financial, personal and professional objectives. Now let's go deeper into those goals.

First of all, take a look at your personal and professional goals and see if they match your financial goals.

As an example, let's say that one of your personal goals was to take a big trip around the world. Would your financial goals support that? If your professional goal was to move into some new role, will that new role support your financial goals? Look around and see if you can tie everything together. See if all your goals have reasons, and check whether they align with each other.

Now, let's go a little bit deeper into your goals. Add more details to each by asking the following question for each: What needs to happen for me to know that I achieved this goal?

Financial goals are usually easy. You want to make a $100,000 a year for example. So if you make a $100,000 a year, you know you achieved your goal. If you didn't make it, you did not achieve the goal.

Another goal you might have is to be recognized. What does that mean to you? A lot of people say, "Oh, I want to be recognized, or I want to change the world." What does that mean? "I want to create a product that affects lots of people." What does that mean? Revisit each one of those goals and list specifically what needs to happen for you to know you achieved it. Get some of those details on paper.

What needs to happen for you to know that you achieved that goal? If your goal was to impact the world, well, impact the world is not very clear. But if you say, "I want 100,000 people using my software," well, that's better. Now you have more clarity, you have a better idea of what you want.

Use the SMART template to better define your goals

To help you get more clarity, you can use the SMART template to define your goals.

SMART is an acronym for Specific, Measurable, Actionable, Relevant and Realistic, and Time-Bound. Your goals should meet all these criteria.

A SMART goal would sound something like this: "I want to have 10,000 followers on Twitter within 12 months." This goal meets all the criteria of the SMART template, beginning with being Specific.

This goal is also Measurable. If you want to have 10,000 followers on Twitter and you now have 2,000 followers on Twitter, you know where you are. Next month, if you only grow by five followers, you know you're not going to achieve your goal. But if you've added about 500 followers or so, you're on the path to achieving your goal. Being measurable is an important part of setting a goal.

Goals need to be Actionable. Very generic goals like, "Oh, I want to impact the world." What does that mean? It's not actionable. But if you say, "I want to create a software product that 10,000 people use," that's actionable, because now you know you have to create a software product. So try to make goals that are actionable; goals you can take action on to achieve your desired result.

Your goals also have to be Relevant and Realistic. They have to be relevant to what you want to do. Your financial goals have to be relevant to what you want to do personally and professionally, and vice versa. You must design your goals so they are realistic, but challenging too. Don't say something like, "Oh, I want to reach 100 people on Twitter." That's a very small number and you probably know you can do it. Make the goals realistic. Don't say you want a million followers on Twitter in the next month because that's not realistic, but the goal has to be a stretch that you actually have to go after and achieve.

Finally, the goals you define have to be Time-bound. They need a deadline. Take a look at your goals to see if they are tied to a time.

Not every single goal needs to make full use of the SMART template. Just keep the acronym in mind when you're developing your goals and include as much of it in each goal as you can. Put details into each goal because that's what is going to help you understand what you need to do to achieve them. The details will help you to keep your focus.

Define your Objectives. In a SMART way!

Now that you have a list of goals, you understand what you want and what you want to do, as well as what you want to earn, it will be a lot easier for you to look for and find the path that will get you there.

What does all this have to do with finding a job? Well, now you know your strengths, all the facets of what you want, and your objectives, you're ready to go look for your dream job. You know the skill set involved in that job, you know how strong you are in certain areas, and you know your financial and professional objectives.

Look at those things again and then take a look at the positions you are interested in. Think how you can use those positions to achieve what you want. It will be a lot easier for you to tell people what you want and what type of job you're looking for, or what you want in a future job, because now you know how strong you are, and you know your objectives.

My friend Eyal was struggling with some projects he was doing on the side. He had a financial discussion with his partner in the project. He was not happy with the way some things were working financially, and he knew he needed to solve the problems or the project wouldn't move forward. But he didn't like the outcome of the discussion. The problem was that Eyal had no clear objectives for what he wanted. He didn't have a clear vision of the results that he wanted out of the negotiation. It was hard for him to negotiate anything. Once he sat down and wrote his objectives for his family, for himself both professionally and personally, he got clarity on his objectives. He knew exactly what he needed to do to negotiate.

This has a lot to do with getting a new job, because getting a new job is all about negotiation. It's all about negotiation with the company, with yourself, with your boss. It's even a negotiation with your family.

Once you have clarity on what it is you want, once you have clarity on your objectives, you can negotiate the best position, the best salary, the best offer for you and for the company. What Eyal did was negotiate a result that was great for him, great for his partner, great for his family, and great for his customers. Once you know what is it that you want, you can negotiate something that's going to be a win, win, win, win, for everyone.

Get clarity on your goals. That's what will make a big difference in you getting the job you want.

Expand your Network

Everyone talks about how important it is for you to have a good network.

A network is a group of people that have similar interests as you and they're working together to achieve similar goals. A network is different from your circle of friends, although some of your friends may be in your network.

A network consists of people -- many are professional, but your network doesn't need to consist of only professionals. A network is a group of people that you can rely on and whom also rely on you. It is a mutual support group. You can form a community of people that have similar interests. We see networks everywhere around us. We see networks around open source projects, technologies, and around meetups and events. All those things are potential places where networks are formed.

There are also great online networking tools. Things like Facebook, LinkedIn, Twitter, Groups.io, Meetup.com and GitHub are all tools that allow you to create your own network. Those tools allows you to reach out and connect with people in your network. But networking is not about online tools. They are all about relationships. The interesting thing about networks is that the relationships are beneficial both for you and for the people in your network.

The best way for you to have a strong network is if people in your network see you as a valuable member of the network. When you bring new information or people to the network or produce exceptional work, you strengthen the network. Then people begin to see you as a valuable, contributing member.

People can be givers or takers. The givers come in and bring things others can benefit from while the takers take more than they give and ultimately drag the network down by trying to benefit themselves. That's why givers tend to grow more than takers or matchers. Matchers are those people that try to do a quid pro quo thing. They give a little bit and they receive a little bit, but the people that grow more are the givers. Because people in the network know how important givers are, they reward them with results and other things of value. A good network is a place where you can be of service to people in the network.

Why is that important? Because once people see you as a valuable member of the network, they're willing to help you grow. That's what we need, right? If we're looking for a better job, a more interesting project in our company or looking to move to another company, you'll find the support in your network. Research shows that 30% of the hires come from other employees[1] referring people from their network to the position. A recruiter told me once that it's 45 times more likely that you get the job if you are referred by someone in your network.

The larger and more active your network is, the more success and the better results you're going to have through your network. If you want to get a new job, expand and strengthen your network. If you want to get a better position inside your company, the fact that you have a good network inside and outside your company is going to help you get a better position.

It doesn't matter what size your network is right now, there are steps you can take to expand it. Just by increasing the size of your network even a little, you'll meet new people and have more opportunities. Each person you bring into your network also brings in new people with fresh contacts and new opportunities. Expanding your network brings exponential results.

Now that you've discovered how to understand your strengths and develop your objectives, we're going to start working on how you get where you want to go. And one of the most important things you can do to move to a better position, is increase your network.

---

[1] 2017 Sources of Hire Report - https://www.silkroad.com/blog/2017-sources-of-hire-report/

Here are the steps you need to take to expand your network. The more of these steps you work on, the bigger your network will grow. And the larger your network is, the better end results you'll have.

Join Facebook and LinkedIn groups related to your desired position

First of all, you're already researching for LinkedIn and Facebook groups that have people who are in your desired position. That's what we did in *Chapter One.* We looked at Facebook groups and we looked at LinkedIn groups that had people in the positions you want.

If you want to be an architect, you research Facebook groups and LinkedIn groups that include architects. Now you need to join these groups. Listen to what the members are saying, what problems they have, what problems they are trying to solve. Listen to what they share. Try to see if there are things in those groups you can help with.

What information can you share; what skills do you have to help them? Remember, we did this in *Chapter one.* You brainstormed this process and now you're going to take action and join those groups and pay attention to see what things you think you can actually apply to those groups.

Join mailing lists of open source projects related to your position

Another thing you can do is look at open source projects that are interesting projects for the position you're looking for.

If you want to be a senior developer, you're looking for open source software that senior developers use and contribute to. If you want to be a designer, you should look at open source projects that designers use and contribute to. Join the mailing lists of those groups. Go on Github and join the projects, so now you can start seeing the people who are part of those projects. Soon you will know who is actually contributing to the projects and who is merely using them.

Learn who they are. Listen to what they are talking about. Ask them questions about what they are doing, about their work, about who they are.

Using Twitter, follow 30 or more influential people

Another thing you can do is go on Twitter right now and follow at least 30 people who are influential in your area.

They might be people who have the same type of position you want, or people that are well known in that position, or they might even be the people who talk about these positions and the people in them.

If you want to be an architect, follow important architects in different programming languages or in different type of projects. If you want to be a cloud architect, go follow some amazing cloud architects on Twitter. Search for them, find them, follow them.

Find meetups in your area and attend in person meetings

The strongest networks rely on personal contact. Find meetups in your area whose members are professionals in the job you want, and during the next meeting plan to make their acquaintance.

Understand what they are doing that's useful. What kind of skills do they have? What kind of suggestions can they give you to improve the skills you have? Go meet people face-to-face and talk with them.

Go where your prospects are. Online and offline

Basically, go where the people from the industry you aspire to meet. Go meet them where they are; online and offline. They can potentially hire or refer you.

There are people who can refer you to other places that can be beneficial to your job search. But when you go there to meet them don't say, "I'm looking for a job. I want to be like you so give me a job." That's not the idea. You go there to meet them; be friends with them. The more of those people you know, the more people you will meet, which means your opportunities will become broader and broader.

It is not about being a taker, but a giver. Meet people and be interested in them, and don't do it out of selfish interests.

Listen. And look for ways to help others

All those people, in all those places, can be part of your network.

They might be people you know, people you've just met, or people you've been interested in knowing for some time since they are a professional in the industry you want to move into.

Don't be a taker that just wants to take everything from the network and run with it. No. Instead, go there to give something to the network. Remember the lists of skills you have? You have good things to share. We're going to talk more in the next chapter about how you can do this.

Right now, though, go find those people on LinkedIn, Facebook, and Meetups. Find them at user groups, at events, seminars, training initiatives, and any other place that you can think of to meet people associated with your desired position. It could be local associations or sporting events, there are lots of places you can meet interesting people from those positions.

In all those places spend time listening, looking around and finding ways to help others. Don't try to just take, you have to be there to help others.

Try to find opportunities to help. Can you help organize events? Put chairs in the right place? Bring in the food? Can you hand out flyers? Any little help you can provide is great. Genuinely offer to help without asking for anything in return.

I'm just suggesting some very basic things, but you can do a lot more than that. You could offer to teach a group of people that don't know how to do some things that are important. You can offer help for a later time, or even help them over the phone in a problem they have, for example. Building your network by offering to help and helping other people to achieve what they want is very strong.

You can get anything you want in life if you help enough people get what they want in life. If you help them get what they want, they're going to help you get what you want.

Spend time helping others – the 5 minute rule

One thing I like to suggest is that you use LinkedIn top networker, Adam Rifkin's Five-Minute Rule[2].

In your network, anytime anyone asks for some kind of favor that you can do in five minutes or less, whatever the favor is, just do it. Help that person. Spend those five minutes. Do it. This one small action is going to be very useful.

If it takes more than five minutes, you might not have the time. It might be just too much work or take too much of your time. If it's something you want to help with and it takes more than five minutes, go ahead and do it, of course. If it's something that's going to take more than five minutes and it's not aligned with your objectives (so you don't want to do it) use the five minutes to direct the person to a better solution. You can introduce them to someone that can help, or suggest a website you know will help them.

If you know enough to help in five minutes, do whatever you can in five minutes and help that person. That will create a positive ripple effect. You help people and they'll help other people. You pay it forward, they pay it forward, and it creates a ripple effect with you at the center of it. That ripple effect comes back to you.

---

[2] The Basics of Power Networking - https://www.linkedin.com/pulse/20130806141819-8244-3-important-things-to-be-mindful-of-as-you-build-your-network/

Expand your Network. Expand your help

Right now, you should be joining Facebook groups and LinkedIn groups whose members already work in the position you want. You'll also want to join open source projects and go to events and meetups. When you do all those things, you get to know more people that already have your position.

Guess what? When someone needs a professional, who do you think they talk to? They talk to someone that's already in that position. Professionals get asked all the time: do you have a friend? Do you know anyone that's looking for a job? Do you know anyone we could hire? The more you expand your network into professionals from the position you want, the more opportunities will open for you. A great network of people can make a huge difference. Not only because they can get you close to people interested in what you want to do, but they might have a better position for you, and they can help you in many other ways, too.

I was talking the other day to Daniel, a friend of mine. Daniel was just beginning his career. He had a lot of difficulties in getting his first job, any job actually. He didn't have any experience and he hadn't studied in the top universities, so he was having a hard time getting started. He didn't know any English and that's an important skill for developers, so he even lacked some basic skills.

But he worked hard to build his network. He started helping on a local Java user group and that helped him build his network. He got to know very good people, amazing people from the Java community. A group of his friends helped him get a temporary job where he could get the experience. That way he could show he was actually capable of doing more complex work on larger projects.

The experience from this temporary job allowed him to land a job he wanted. Because he had a good network, people worked with him to get him into a position that would jumpstart his career. Having a good network is a big push!

Another friend of mine, who is also named Daniel, was working on an open source project while also working to extend his network. He knew no English, but a large company saw the work he was doing on the open source project and wanted to hire him. It was an international company and they required English. He said, "I can't take this job. I'm sorry. I don't have any skills in English." Instead of accepting his answer, they replied that it was not a problem. They decided to teach him English. They paid for the instructor. And waived the requirement to know English for the moment.

Today, Daniel is an amazing open source developer that works in a large company on very interesting projects. And he speaks English. All because of his network. People knew the good work he was doing, and helped him get where he wanted to be.

Working on improving your network, even if you expand it just a little, is going to be a big help to you. If you are looking for a new job or don't have the luxury of waiting because you desperately need a new job, the best thing you can do... the most important thing you can do... is expand your network. Any small growth you manage to achieve in your network makes a difference, and is going to help you get the job of your dreams.

Promote Yourself

Just having a good network is not enough, though, because if people don't know what it is that you know, what it is that you're good at, or what you're interested in, how can they help you? Promoting yourself is not about saying, "Look at me." Promoting yourself is not about becoming a well-known superstar. It could be that, too, but promoting yourself is not about making or marketing false claims.

Promoting yourself is very simple. Share what you know. To share what you already know makes a huge difference for your career. You don't need to learn new things. You don't need to become a master of anything. You don't need to be a different you to be able to share what you know. It's always about what you already know. If you look at the list of your strengths, you define for yourself what you know. You start from the strengths you have.

There's a lot of things you're very good at; a lot of the things you have experience with. A lot of things you love to do, and because you love to do them, you are good at doing them. Or things that you're very good at, and because you're very good at them, you love to do them. You can share those things because they are things you know. You've been doing them. You do them in your free time. You do them in your work. Sometimes you've even done them since you were a child.

All those skills you have will help you share what you know with others, with people that don't yet have the skills. Once you start sharing what you know, you become valuable to your network. And the more valuable you are to your network, the more your network helps you become better and better. Your network helps you get new jobs, because they see your value!

People are interested in helping people that help them. Not only this, but if you share what you know, more people will know that you are good at that. More people will know you are the qualified person for the position they have. More people will know you are the right person to work on their team. Because they know you are the right person to work on their team, they will suggest you to their company.

Then you get a better, more interesting position because people know who you are and they trust you. Getting the best job possible is a question of trust. When they trust you because they know who you are, it's a lot easier for you to get the jobs you deserve.

So, how do you promote yourself the right way?

First: understand it is not about you!

First things first. The very first thing you have to understand about sharing what you know is, "it's not about you."

Really, it's not about you. No one cares about you. No one cares about me, either. People care about how you can help them get what they want. That is the truth.

Every time you share, you have to understand that you're not sharing to show how great you are. You're not sharing to show the amazing skills you have. You're not sharing to know how knowledgeable you are.

You're sharing because you're helping other people get what they need to get; what they want to get. If you understand that sharing is about them and not about you, that it's about listening. It's about what they need. It's not about you. Then you put sharing in the right perspective. You're not sharing to be the most amazing person, you're sharing to help other people achieve what they want.

Improve your social media profiles; make them more professional

The second thing you can do to improve your sharing is to improve your social media profile, right now.

It's something that might take half an hour to an hour. Go to all your social media profiles, your Twitter, Facebook, LinkedIn, go to all and improve them. Upload a nicer picture, add a description. You want people to see you as a valuable member of the community, and a valuable member of the community is not someone that keeps talking about himself. Instead, they talk about what the community needs. So go improve your social profiles. Improve the description, improve the pictures and follow the right people.

The profile picture should show you at your best! Look at how other professionals present themselves. The banner at the top should be related to what you will talk about in your account. Show you among peers. Show something related to what you want. Make it count.

The description is important to get people to be interested in what you have to say. Make it NOT about you! The description should be about what people are going to get if they follow you and become your friend. Look at your strengths again; find the things you're good at.

Are you going to help them become better runners? Are you going to help them become better writers of code? Are you going to help them understand artificial intelligence or big data? What are the things you know how to do? Do you want to help them communicate better with other people? Can you help them become better architects? Whatever it is, find the strengths you have. Find the skills you have and figure out what you're going to discuss in your social media profiles.

Who you follow will give you the content you need so you can share, and also will tell others who you hang out with and who you admire. If the only people you follow on Twitter or Facebook are the ones you exchange jokes with or bash politicians with, you can't help anyone else because you have no good content. Remove all those people and, instead, follow positive people. Positive people bring good information to you, so you can share good information with your community and network. Again, that makes you more valuable to your network. Be sure to remove, hide or make private all the bad taste jokes, rants, and other things that are negative.

Also, follow influential people in your area of interest. Share what they are talking about. Reply to their posts. Strike a conversation. Sharing content with your network from top influencers in your interest area make you more interesting to the people in your network.

Being more interesting to your network with improved social media profiles -- especially on LinkedIn, Facebook and Twitter -- means you are more valuable to anyone who wants to hire you. You'll be someone that's bringing a positive influence and positive content to your network.

Write small articles about the skills you are good at

Choose a couple of the skills you're very good at that are relevant to the position you want and write a blog post or article.

But don't write any random thing. Keep in mind that all the efforts you are making are about the position you want. Go back to the list of skills you developed in Chapter One and choose things that are relevant.

It can be a one-page article, or even less, three or four paragraphs that talk about how to improve on that skill. Mention things that are talked about on the internet so people can gain more in-depth information by searching the internet and reading more about that skill. Or tell a story from your experience that helped you improve the skill.

Write several articles if you can that cover the skills you have that can help other people get what they want. These articles can help people become better at what they do.

You want to be around people who are already working in the position you want. What kind of information do those people need? Just because someone is a senior developer doesn't mean they are good at everything. There are things you are very good at that they aren't. So talk about the things you're very good at and help them become better by reading your article.

Your article should not be about you. It is not saying, "Oh my skills are great. Come hire me because I'm great." This is not about you. Talk about them. Talk about how they can improve their own skills. How they can be better, how they can become better developers. How they can become better architects. How they can become better designers.

Write about your experience with open source software

You can also write about open source software. Remember how we looked at open source software in *Chapter One* and then in *Chapter Three* we joined some open source software groups? Well, now go write something about those software projects.

Explain to others how that particular open source software can help them in their positions. Tell them how using that open source project can help their company solve problems or how it can help them create a better team. You're bringing valuable information to people when you explain how an open source software tool works; information they can use to improve their projects. You'll become valuable to their projects.

Write articles. You can write one or two articles a week. If you are out of a job, you should do more frequently, so, every couple of days write a short article. It doesn't need to be long; a short article will help you when you publish it on LinkedIn, Facebook and Twitter.

Those experiences you had with open source are going to help you show everyone else that you have the skills necessary for that position you want.

Answer questions from members in your groups

Another thing you can do since you're participating in groups on Facebook and LinkedIn as well as some of the meetups and open source groups is answer questions from people in those groups. When you see questions, get involved and answer, be helpful. Suggest new ideas or a new way to solve a problem they have.

It's not about you. Do not talk about you. Help them solve the problem or problems they have, whatever they are.

Share what you ALREADY know and what you are good at

Sharing does not mean learning new things. You can if you have the time, if you're not in a hurry, if you don't need a job as fast as possible.

You can always learn new things and then share them, but right now, share what you already know, share the things you're good at, because doing so will attract the people to you that need that information, that need someone like you who already knows that stuff.

Let me show some easy ideas on how you can start sharing!

Post articles to Medium.com

Now that you're writing those short articles, post them on Medium.com. Medium is a great place to post articles because it doesn't require you to have a full blog with lots of posts. People can find and read your posts easily.

Even if you just have one article in Medium.com, people can find that article and talk to you and see what are you doing. You will also be able to promote it freely, with no fear of showing your new and empty or old and outdated blog. That makes Medium a great place for you to (re)start blogging.

Eventually, you might get your own blog site, but right now, all you need is to have a few articles. That's going to make a difference already. Medium is free, you should go create an account and begin posting right now. Just go to the site; it's very easy.

To improve things, you can look around first to see what tags you should put in the article so the right people get to see it.

It's also great if you already have a blog. Just re-post your articles on Medium, after posting to your blog. That will expand who gets to see it, and will help you reach a new audience.

Get started, even a single article can make a big difference!

Post articles to LinkedIn

Go to LinkedIn and post the article there, too. Reposting your content to LinkedIn is simple and takes no effort. And improves your profile a lot!

You can then promote your article to the groups you joined, that have people who already have the position you want. Some will see it and connect with you.

LinkedIn it is a great place to post articles because there are a lot of headhunters that use LinkedIn. They keep looking at people and read their articles to see if they have the skills needed for a particular job. The fact that you're posting articles on LinkedIn will attract headhunters that have positions that require the skills you wrote about in your article.

After you wrote your articles, reposting them to LinkedIn is so simple, there is no reason not to do it. It will attract the right positions to you.

Do presentations

Also, another thing you can do is presentations. This is scary, so, how can you do presentations in an easy, non scary way?

Remember, it's about sharing things you already know. It's about the things you're already good at. Those things are your strengths. Talking about what you know is easier.

You can start by going to places that are easier. Present for your friends at your work. Present at the university you studied, for a small class. Go to technical schools or high schools that teach computer programming.

Another thing is to do small presentations. Instead of preparing an hour-long presentation, work on a 5 minute or 10 minute lightning talk. Those require just one single topic, that you can present anywhere.

So where do you give presentations? There are lots of places. The one I would start with is a nearby university or a school (e.g.: the one you studied at). Try to do it for a class that is learning skills for the position you want.

But, there are other places too!

At local meetups

You should present to your local user group or at a local meetup.

You may wonder whether people want you to present for their meetup. Well, if you want to present an hour-long presentation, people from your meetup will say, "Well, we don't know who this guy is." You know, "He's been here once. We have no idea what he knows..." "Let's bring in other speakers that we know better," and then you don't have a chance to speak.

But if you come to the meetup and say, "Look, guys. I have this short presentation about an open source project that I know about," or, "about this article that I published on LinkedIn." That's easy to say, right? So it's a short presentation. "It's a five-minute presentation. I'm just going to talk about three mistakes people make." "It's very short, it's just about this open source project and the very important skill that architects need." Make sure you get clear on the benefit to the audience.

Then you can ask: "Can I present between speakers?" Or, "Can I speak before the main speaker starts? I'll start when people are still coming in, so I won't take but a few minutes from the other speaker." If you ask it like this, you know, five-minutes is not a problem. Most meetups will allow people to speak for five minutes. It's a short time. It's not going to bother their schedule, and if the presentation is bad, it's okay. People not going to get upset because it's just a five-minute presentation.

That will get you the slot, and then you will present a great presentation, not a bad one! Stick to the time allotment they gave you. If you have five minutes, then do five minutes. If they gave you ten minutes, speak for ten minutes. Do not go over your time allotment. If they gave you three minutes, do it in three minutes. Respect the organizers.

Once you present, even this tiny little presentation, this little three to five minutes you are speaking means everyone around you is going to know what skills you have. That should get a few people coming up to you during the break, or at the end of the event to say, "Hey, I liked your presentation. That's an interesting thing you said," and then you can strike up a conversation.

Doing presentations is an amazing way for you to get in front of people. Then, once you do this presentation at a meetup, you can write an article about the results of the presentation. And then you can develop a presentation about the article you wrote.

Now that you've done a small presentation you can say to your audience, "I only had five minutes today, but next week I'm going to repeat this presentation in a longer format on a webinar on YouTube. If you want to see it, follow me on Twitter and I can send you the link." Or, "Give me your email and I can send you an invite for next week."

Now you have people interested in what you have to say because they watched you talk for five minutes. You can also ask the organizers for a chance to speak more in the future.

On YouTube

Doing a presentation on YouTube is great, too. All you need is your cell phone camera or your computer and you can record short videos to go on YouTube in order to connect with the people in your network.

And YouTube is great to post existing content in new format. You write an article on LinkedIn and then record a video; then you post about the article and you post about the YouTube video. Then you get the article and publish it to medium.com with the link to your video. You also publish the slides to Slideshare.com. All these methods are using the same content, but they are different content, because they have different formats. You can then post on LinkedIn all the content you created, making your profile even more interesting.

People prefer to learn content in different ways. So, all those formats are going to add a lot of value to your network. Start getting more comfortable with this and remember, it can be done in a very short amount of time.

At local companies

Once you're confident with this, another interesting thing you can do to get the job you want is to offer to do those presentations for companies.

Make a list of the companies you would like to work for. What do you think they'd do if you sent an email saying, "I'd like a job at your company." They'd say they don't know who you are. So you send HR a resume. Do you think this will help you get a job there?

It might work, depending on who you sent the message to and how good your resume is, but there's a very small chance that it will work. The problem with this approach is that it's about you. YOU want the job...

But if you do things the other way around and try to add value to them, they will be more interested! Send an email to the appropriate person in the company and explain that you have this content (articles, videos, etc) about this amazing skill that software developers need. Show how that skill can help their teams or their projects. And then, offer to present to their teams about this skill, for free. Make it about them, and not about you.

You can offer to present during lunch time or after hours or online, and you can offer to present at as many companies as you can think of. Send the emails. They might say, "No, not interested," but that's not the same thing as saying, "We don't want to hire you."

Since it's valuable for them, for their teams, it's a lot easier for them to say, "That's a cool thing. It's a cool topic. We'd love to know more about it. You can come." Some companies have strong policies about this and will not allow you to present. But a lot of companies, a lot of developers, especially smaller ones, would love to listen. You can offer to do a remote presentation for a group of two, three or four. So, you don't have to get management approval, just a developer that's willing to listen. That way you'll begin making connections inside the companies you are interested in working for.

Many times the person that will offer you a job or invite you to come to interview is watching a presentation you're giving at a meetup. Offer to do a presentation at their company. During your presentation, you clearly offer to come to any company interested, that you can repeat it for their teams in their offices. You can say, "I'm very interested in Java 10, and I'd love to do a presentation about it for your company. The one I did here just covered the most important parts, but I can do a much more thorough presentation for your company if you'd like."

That's an amazing way for you to get in. Because once you get inside the company and deliver a presentation, and people like your presentation, you can always say, "I'm keeping an eye out for a more challenging position and more interesting projects to work on. If you have anything available here I'd love to send in an application." Now they know who you are. Now they trust you. Now it's not about hiring someone they've never seen. Trust makes all the difference in a hiring process.

Giving a presentation and making time for the companies you'd like to work for is a great way to show your value.

Work on a company's open source project

There are other ways to show your value if you don't want to do presentations. Many developers would rather work on the company's software. You can work WITH them long before you actually work FOR them!

A lot of people get nervous when they come into an interview and the interviewer says, "You have to answer those questions and write code here on the whiteboard." That's terrible, isn't it? Why do people do this? They do this because they want to eliminate candidates. So instead of going down this path, what if you did something else?

Before you start applying for jobs and get asked to come in for an interview, make a list of the companies you are interested in working for and see if they have any open source software. Consider working for them for free on their open source projects. Become one of their contributors. You're showing your value to them. Now they'll think, "We need a developer and we already know this guy works very well. He's working on our open source project. We should hire him." That happens all the time. If you do some work for the company you want to work for, they are going to see your value even before they call you in for an interview.

With open source being so spread out everywhere, absolutely every company has a one or more open source projects.

Do you want to work for the big companies like Netflix, DropBox or Google? Anyone else? Oracle, Red Hat or Microsoft? All the big ones have a long list of interesting open source projects. Even Disney has amazing open source projects! Do you want to work for the small ones? A lot of startups have open source projects.

If you come in and start contributing to their open source projects, you show your value way before they invite you in for an interview. When they invite you in for an interview you can say, "Why do I need to do code on the whiteboard, when I have code committed to your project, in your product." The truth is that you won't even have to say that. They will call you knowing it.

There's so many open source projects out there that could use your skills. A lot of projects need you.

Promote Yourself. The right way

In short, all those ideas -- doing a presentation for the company; bringing technology, new ideas, and solutions for their employees; showing how their employees can improve their skills; working on an open source project or just helping out with the open source project -- are all amazing ways you can show your value to a company way before they call you in for an interview.

Once they call you for an interview, they will already know and trust you. And then, the magic happens. They won't try to reject you, they will try to hire you. Sometimes, they might even open up a position for you! I've seen this happen many times, companies who are so interested in what you are doing that they create a position for you, so you can do what you do best for them.

The important thing about sharing what you know is not simply coming and talking about how great you are. Actually, that's not it at all. This is the wrong approach. The way for you to become known the right way, the way where people want you to work for them, is to make it about them, not you. Put your time, especially if you're unemployed, into being of service to the companies you'd like to work for. Become important to them, and that will help them become interested in you.

Understand it's not about you. Understand that you can easily improve your social media profile, but improve it in a way that people see the value you bring for them. When you understand this, you'll create content that's important to them: small articles that you publish on meetup, small articles that you publish on medium.com, or those you publish on LinkedIn. You answer questions. You participate on open source projects. You can contribute when you know how to help the project become better. A lot of times you don't even need to contribute code. You can help with documentation.

You can do a presentation about the open source project. So you share what you already know, and that makes a big difference.

Then, once you've done that, do some presentations in your groups and on YouTube. The best companies host presentations that help their employees become better staff members. If you present to them you'll get to know interesting people in the industry and even come across someone who wants to hire you. Go work on open source projects for those companies, because in putting your time to their service, you're showing them the value you have to offer before they call you to interview. If you keep these things in mind, they will help you share the right way.

A friend of mine, Edson, was fired from his company. He was already sharing what he knew. He was sharing everything he knew about containers, and sharing everything he knew about DevOps, sharing all the time. He was also working on open source projects. He was fired by his company, and a multinational company saw all the work he had done related to containers and DevOps, and hired him. He didn't have to send a resume out, people went after him and said, "We want you. We want you to come to work for us."

Sharing what you know is important. Edson did this. He learned how to share the right way. He learned to share in a way that helps others achieve what they want. It was not about him talking about himself, it was not about him throwing a party for himself. Rather, he was always helping others achieve what they wanted. That made all the difference. Today he is the director of a multinational company and has moved to another country. All this because he learned how to share the right way.

Once you start sharing in the right way you become important to your community. You become important to your network, and your network will want you to work for them. Makes sense?

Get Quality Interviews

Interviews are the way we get new jobs. But not every interview is a great interview.

A lot of times we send resumes, we get our friends to suggest us, or we try to reach out to all kinds of different companies. We talk with headhunters. Then we get all those crappy interviews where the position is not a good fit for us, or the company wants us to do all these crazy things to prove in one hour our lifetime value… The sad truth is that you only have a 1.2% chance of getting a job through an online application[3].

There are two types of interviews or two paths an interview can take.

One is the path of rejection. That's what most interviews are. You send a resume and someone looks at the resume and says, "Oh, this guy doesn't know what we want." They throw the resume away. Then maybe it's a good resume, so its sent on to another person. That person says, "Okay, let me talk with this guy. Let me actually ask the hard questions to see what he's worth." They ask you these hard questions and wait to see if you answer them correctly. If you don't, that person says, "He didn't answer right. Reject him."

You may even have answered right but then another person gets involved and says, "He may have not made mistakes, but let me make sure this guy knows his stuff." Then they call you to do weird exercises on a whiteboard or some other crazy exercises. And they find out reasons to reject you.

This whole interview process is designed to reject you.

---

[3] Statistic provided by Gerry Crispin of Career Xroads, as mentioned by Charlotte Weeks in - https://www.linkedin.com/pulse/20140925150631-6561910-you-have-a-1-2-chance-of-getting-a-job-through-an-online-application-how-to-increase-your-odds/

The second path an interview can take is completely opposite. It's the path of acceptance. Someone from the team knows who you are and suggests your name for the available position. Now, you are on a path where they trust you because the team trusts you already. They know you.

They know you because they're working with you. They know you because they watched your videos on YouTube. They saw your code on an open source project. You are even part of the company's open source project. They trust you already. The whole process is, "Okay, we trust this guy. Let's walk him through the process so we can hire him."

The interview process is made to hire you.

On the interview process made to reject you, candidates interviewed from an external source, like sending the resume, 1 in 33 get the job. But on the interview process made to hire you, candidates that are referred internally, 1 in 9 get the job[4].

Which one of these interview paths do you want to be part of? I think I know your answer. But also take into account that when you're in the interview process that's made to reject you, someone else is going through the process parallel to you where the company wants to hire them. They want to reject you because they want to hire someone else. Of course you want to be in the path that's made to hire you. You want to be the person they want to hire.

If you are on the path where they want to hire you, sometimes companies will stretch to hire you. We saw in the story of Daniel where the company actually paid an English teacher to teach him the English language. If you are on the path to being rejected, they'd say, "No English. Reject." You'll not even be called for an interview. But Daniel was on the path where people wanted to hire him, so they found ways to accept him.

Every time you're doing this, every time you're on the path to being hired, people want you in the team, so they will find ways to solve whatever the problem is that could

---

[4] 2017 Sources of Hire Report - https://www.silkroad.com/blog/2017-sources-of-hire-report/

stand in the way of you being hired. They will be open to discussing all possibilities. They can even eliminate or downplay crazy interview processes.

It goes even beyond that. Many, many times I've seen companies create new positions because they want to hire the person they are interviewing. 80000 Hours career website says that "the best opportunities are less competitive because they are hidden away, often at small but rapidly growing companies, and personalised to you."[5]

I was in a situation like this once. I was hired by a company that did not have a position for me at that time, so they created one. It took 4 months, but they created a position just so they could hire me.

The more you can get the company on the path to hire you, the better for you. And, the better for them, because they will be hiring someone perfect for the position! Interviews like that are quality interviews.

Get interviews in all those places

How do you do this? How do you actually get quality interviews?

By now, you are working on social media, you're working on an Open Source project, you're giving presentations, you're going to meetings, and you're actually visiting companies to present what you know for those companies.

In all those places, try to get quality interviews. When you meet new people, and they trust you, they understand your skills, they will suggest you to their company.

Let me walk through a few ideas that could make this easier to happen.

Offer free consultations about your best skills

An amazingly effectively idea is to offer free consultations for companies.

---

[5] All the best advice we could find on how to get a job - https://80000hours.org/career-guide/how-to-get-a-job/

Let's say you're great at Java migration. You migrate from one version of Java to the next. You've done this on lots of projects. You've done it on some open source projects. You've done this in your company. So you are great at this. That's a skill (you have done it) and not just knowledge. So, offer a free consultation. In a presentation or even in a conversation, you can say, "Hey, amazing that you are migrating your Java app! I'm very good at migrating from one Java version to the next, and I've been doing this for my company for a long time. I'm willing to help with your project. I'm going to come in and we're going to spend a day (or an hour or two hours) looking at your code and I'll show you how you can migrate from one version to the next."

Or you're very good at doing REST. When someone says they are building a new API, you can say, "That's great, I'm doing a lot of REST APIs on my projects. I'm willing to come in and take a look at your projects to see what you are already doing. I'll do an assessment. I'm going to tell you what works -- and what doesn't, and both the good and not so good things about REST."

Or you're very good at communication. Then, in talking with someone you learn their company is bad at communication. You can offer, "I'm going to come in and give you a free consultation. I'm going to come in and talk with your developers for an afternoon, and I'm going to help them become better communicators."

You can offer a free consultation for anything you are good at. Then you can come in and talk with people, you can help them improve in whatever it is you are very good at.

You're giving them a free consultation, so while you're there, check to see if they have positions available. If they don't have anything, that's okay. You learned something about the company and you learned something about the people. They trust you. Even though they don't have anything right now, maybe they will in the future.

Free consultations are an excellent way to help them and to learn more about the company, as well as give you more experience in your field. After you did a few of those, you can honestly say, "I've been doing consultations for several companies about this." You help them. Gain experience. And it will make you more valuable to everyone around you.

Free consultations are a great way for you to get your foot in the door at a company and to meet the person who might be interested in hiring you.

Offer to do a project for them

Another great way of getting your foot in the door with a company is to offer to do a project for them. Potentially free.

Let's say you're looking at the open source project and you notice that there is a feature missing, and there's a lot of people asking for it. You can offer to implement that feature. Just make sure this is something the developers want done, and that they don't have time to do. So, you can put your time in. Then, you go and learn all you need to learn. And then show you are capable of doing it.

Or, let's say you want to work as a designer. You can take a look at their company's website and offer, "Your website is lacking in certain areas so I redesigned this particular page to show you how I can help."

You can do those as little projects. In a great blog post, Raghav Haran proposed what he called these "pre-interview projects"[6], projects you do for the company before the interview process even starts.

Those projects can actually create the opportunity for you to get invited for an interview. But they also can be used during the interview itself. You could say, "Since I'm being interviewed here, I decided to go ahead and do this project for you guys that solves the problem you're having just to show that I'm able to solve problems for you."

Those are ways for you to show your value even before you walk into the room for the interview.

---

[6] How to Get Any Job You Want (even if you're unqualified) - https://medium.com/the-mission/how-to-get-any-job-you-want-even-if-you-re-unqualified-6f49a65f5491

Once you complete the project, you send them the project, and they show it to someone at the company, someone that can have some influence. People have sent those to CEOs and CIOs. But you can send to a friend or someone you met in an event. And when you come in for the interview, they want to hire you because they already see your value. You're not on the path of rejection. You're on the path that says, "Hey, this guy does a great job. Let's find a way to hire him." The path of acceptance.

Get Quality Interviews. To be hired, not rejected

Both pre-interview projects and free consultations are examples of the same thing: you come in, you solve a problem for the company, so they trust you.

"This is a great developer. She came here, solved a problem. We trust her. We want to hire her." You get yourself on the path to being hired, not on the path to being rejected.

Remember that you only have a 1.2% chance of getting a job through an online application, and more than 30% of jobs are filled because someone internal referred them to the company. So, it is sending resumes or replying to job boards that you will get the best jobs. You get the best positions because someone from the team suggested you as a great fit for the position.

If you're helping people in your network, those people will suggest you to their bosses because they trust you, they see what you're doing; they see that you're solving problems for them.

When you give up your time, it shows a company you would be a good employee. An employee that puts effort into solving a company's problems is the exact type of employee they are looking for. If you put the work into doing this, what's going to happen? You'll be seen as the type of person they want.

By the way, this strategy works not only if you want a new job; it also works great if you want a different job in the company you currently work for. Moving does not mean that you need to leave your company.

If you want to work for a different team or on a different project, let's say the team that's developing sophisticated, innovative applications no one else has done yet, it's the same thing: go do some work first. Show that team you can be valuable right now even before you're part of the team. You have what it takes. And you can make sure they see your value and trust you before the time comes when they should consider you for the team. If they trust you, they will consider you. Then the going will be a lot easier for you.

Even internally, where it's not really an "interview", this is the type of conversation you want. In all cases, you should look for an interview where people want to hire you - to bring you to their team. You should avoid interviews where people want to reject you, that's time consuming and emotionally taxing.

For all the persons being interviewed who they want to reject, there's someone being interviewed who they want to hire. You can be that person they want to hire. If you work on these strategies you're going to get quality interviews. You're going to be called in for interviews where people want to hire you. There's going to be a much larger chance of being hired. Forty-five times larger, because you're being suggested by someone rather than sending in a resume. That's the right way of doing it.

Once you understand that, what do you do? Go to as many events as you can. Go to as many Facebook groups as you can. Offer openly; say, "I have a free week next week. I can visit five companies next week." Work hard to get an invitation one day next week from someone that wants you to come and do a free consultation. Go there, do your best. Offer everything you have, don't hide anything.

That's another pro-tip. A lot of people say, "I'm just going to do a little bit, because if I don't do everything, they will need me. They'll hire me." That's the wrong approach.

Others think that if you solve it all, the company will just take what you did and say goodbye. Well, if they are that unethical, it's actually better for you that you don't work for them! So, don't be afraid. Go there and give all you got. Solve the problem as much as you can. Give everything you have. If you give them everything you have, you can always go get more, you can always learn more and have more to give. But if you just give a little taste, that taste is not going to be enough to show your value. Then they are not going to hire you. Give everything you have, be helpful to people. That will put you on the path of them wanting to hire you. That is the way for you to get the best jobs.

I've seen this many, many times. Developers come for a presentation, or a meeting, or some consulting. They do their best, and give it all. This results in everyone being impressed. The team discusses internally, and call them in. And they get offered a job. They may go through some interviews, usually mostly to meet the people. Once they get the job, that's when the job is posted online.

You got that? I'll repeat it...

After they get offered the job (and accepted it!), the job is posted online!

This means that amazing position, the perfect position you found online, that you got excited and you carefully prepare your resume for. Yes, that one you thought would be your big chance, because you have all the qualifications for it. Well, it does not exist. Someone else has already been hired, before you could even see it.

The best option is for you to be the person that is called in, because the best positions in the industry are offered to people the team or the hiring person already trusts.

You want to be the person that's offered that perfect position before it is taken. How do you do this? Lets recap the whole process.

1. **Find your strengths** and list your skills. This is how you create value.

2. Next, **define clear objectives** for what you want and how you'll get it. Be very clear, very detailed about what you want. If you don't know what you want, how can you get it?
3. Then, **expand your network**. Use social media, write articles, create YouTube videos, and join open source projects and meetup groups. Go help people in all those places. Bring your value to your network.
4. **Promote yourself** by sharing what you know in the right way. It's not about you. Share it to help them. Share to solve problems for people around you. That adds value to your network.
5. **Get quality interviews** by offering value even before you are called in. That will get you called in first.

Share what you know is valuable to your network and to the companies you want to work for. Your message is valuable. The skills you have, that you are great at, are valuable, too. Go share with your network; make it more powerful. The more you share what you know, the better your network is going to be and the more people will trust you. And once they trust you, you'll find yourself on the acceptance path. The 'we want to hire you!' path. You'll get quality interviews because they trust you and they've seen how you are in the network. And because they've seen that you know your stuff. They see your strengths, and how you can help them.

At this point you may be thinking that this could work… If you had several years to do it! Well, let me assure you: this process doesn't need to take long.

Of course, if you're not desperate right now, if you have a job and you just want to move to a better position you can take your time and work on every strategy. The more time you have, the deeper you can go.

But if you don't have a job right now, if you have been fired, if your company went bankrupt or anything along these lines, and you're in a desperate situation, you can do all the steps in the process in a short amount of time.

There is no magic. It's a lot of work, that's why it works. And, it comes from what you already know. That too is why it works. You are not creating things out of nothing. You are carefully collecting what you have, and using it to move you forward towards where you want to go.

Doing even a little bit of this is better than doing none at all. Do a little bit of those five steps everyday. You get clarity on your strengths. You get clarity on your objectives. You increase your network by one or two people each day. You share what you know a little bit each day. You go get whatever interview you're able to get from that sharing. You do this every day and do it over and over and over and over again. In a short amount of time, you can get a much more interesting and much better job.

And once you do, you have a choice to keep moving. Up.

Next steps...

Congratulations for working on improving your career. Now that you are doing it, what's next?

If you are a professional developer, and you are struggling with getting your career moving I'd like to help you. Following my Dad's example, I've been helping developers for more than 20 years to grow their careers and to work on the best projects and teams.

You picked up this book to help you move, to go after your dream job. You are doing your part, and I'd like to be there to help you.

Are you in any of those situations?

- A professional developer with several years in your career...
- Would like to be recognized for your qualities as a developer...
- Do you feel stuck and unhappy with how your career is going...
- Would you like to work on a dream job, in an amazing team...
- Are you worried about keeping up with technology...
- Do you feel unfocused and overwhelmed...

Schedule a free conversation with me. In it, I'll help you:

- Get clarity on your dreams and objectives for the next 12 months
- I'll help you eliminate the biggest issue that prevents you from growing
- Together we will create a plan and a path for you to get where you want to be

This is totally free, no strings attached. If you would like to consider working with me on a program that can make you grow even faster, we can discuss about that too.

Ready to change your career? Schedule a conversation and get cool bonus for this book at: http://jav.mn/bestdevjobever

There are times you need to move because you don't have a choice, perhaps because you've been fired. Sometimes you move because you have a choice. You want to grow or you simply want better circumstances. These are two different situations. Let's discuss both so you can choose the right ideas and techniques and path for each of them should they ever occur.

Moving because I DO have a Choice

First, let's talk about moving because you still have a choice. When does that happen? Well, you have a choice when you are still working, you're doing a good job, no one is going to fire you, your job is not at risk. You have a choice right now to stay in your position or to move to another position; to stay in your company or to move to another company. This is the best situation ever. You should always be ready, you should always be at your best so you can always have a choice.

Having a choice is the best position to be in. I like to say that having a choice is like being a professional soccer player. The professional soccer player wears a team shirt until the day he doesn't. He works hard, he trains hard, he plays hard, he wants to be the best soccer player on that team. Until the day he can become the best soccer player on another team. He changes teams when he's at his top. He doesn't let his game go downhill just because he wants to move; he's the best, and he wants to move and become the best again. If he wasn't the best, he might not have the chance to play for another team.

That's what you should do, you should work to be the best person in your team right now. You might not like your company, it might not give you a lot of opportunity, it might not be the exact project you want, but while you're working for that company, be your best. Be the best you can be for that project or for that team. If you have a choice, it's because you're already working, you're not running the risk of being laid off. While you have a choice, go do everything we've been talking about in this book.

Understand your strengths, understand how you can improve your strengths because you have time. Get clear on what your real objectives are and why your company doesn't offer a means to fulfill those objectives. Go expand your network, share what you know. All those things are going to put you in a position where you are the best you can be. What I've frequently seen is that once you are the best you can be, opportunities open everywhere, including inside your own company. You're going to see interesting projects your company is doing that you didn't have the opportunity to work on before because no one knew how good you are.

Now that they know, you can see new opportunities, you can get a raise, you can get a better position, you can become a leader, you can move from one department to the next. Improving inside your company is an amazing way to improve because you're not risking anything, nor are you burning bridges. You're actually improving because you want to offer your very best to your company. You want to be what they need. That is a great way for you to grow, you can do this.

By doing the steps that are outlined in this book, you can become a better and better person inside your company. And because you're better inside the company, you're going to get offers to go work for other organizations.

You can always listen to what they offer. Say, "I'm very interested in talking to you guys, but I love the work I do. My company supports me. I'm doing a great job there. I want to be the best I can be right there, or here. You better make me a great offer because I'm not leaving my company for nothing." You are in a better situation, a better position to negotiate if you are a better you - if you are a better person for your company.

By the way, it becomes a lot more interesting at your company if you are the best. If you are the best and they're a good company, they will want you to stay. They'll find ways for you to stay.

Sometimes, it's not about finding ways for them to make you stay. Let's say, you were working for a great company, you love what you do, but you want to work on artificial intelligence and your company's not interested. You tried some projects, but they're not interested. Nothing is going to happen in your company with artificial intelligence. Then you get an offer from another company. You might want to leave because you want to do something different, or better, or whatever, and your company might not be the place you want to stay since you can't move in the direction of your work interests.

Moving in this case is not burning bridges. You can tell your boss, "I'm going to another position because this company doesn't want to work with artificial intelligence, and I do."

I have a friend that was in this situation. He told his boss he was going to leave because there was nothing he could do to improve his situation inside the company. You know what the boss did? They created a new department, an innovation department, so he could have a better position inside his own company. There are things a company will do if they value you and see the value you bring to them. They'll find ways to keep you. I've got friends who have moved out of a company they worked for, but they still remain in contract with the company to this day. They still do parts of the work they enjoyed while working for the company because they did not burn bridges.

I left my company and then came back. Twice. For different companies. You can leave without burning bridges when people see you're moving to a position because they cannot offer anything similar.

If you have the time, be the best you can be, right where you are. Don't say things like: "My company, my project is terrible. I don't like my project. My company is not evolving. There's nothing for me to do here. I hate it." Well, that is a bad attitude. No one wants to put a person that hates his job into another job. I won't hire someone that hates his job. I want to hire someone that even though his job is limiting, he's doing his best. Of course, there are situations where your job is terrible. We're going to talk about not having a choice, but if you have a choice because your job is not terrible and you're only disgruntled because it could be better, well, be the best, be your best. Doing so will actually open up opportunities.

If your company doesn't have any specific things you can do, create something. If they don't want to start a new project, find ways you can prove your skills. Remember the list of skills you created in *Chapter One* where you listed your skills and you listed the skills you need to have for the position you want to have? Well, which skill is missing?

Go practice the skill you're missing in your company today. There's lots of opportunities for you to do this. Practice negotiation or communication skills, go discuss things with your boss. There's nothing for you to lose. You don't want to work there anyway, so go have a productive discussion with your boss; do not bash him. Have conversations with him and other people inside the company. Expand your network where you are.

All those things are going to be amazing ways for you to get more opportunities both inside and outside of your company. Go do these things right now even if you don't like your job, they are doable. You can improve and be better by doing those things right now.

Because you have a choice; you can choose if and when to move.

Moving because I DON'T have a Choice

What is it you need to do when you don't have a choice?

First, what does it mean we don't have a choice? Well, there's several different things. The obvious one is that you've been fired. If you've been fired, you don't have a choice. It's gone, you're out. Your company went bankrupt or it is in such a dire financial situation that you know you're going to be fired or the company is going to be bankrupt at any minute. You don't have a choice because of that.

Or you don't have a choice because you work in a very negative place. You work in a place that is damaging you. It's emotionally damaging. It could be financially damaging or professionally damaging because it isn't ethical. Are they lying to the customer or the investors, or the company's doing something illegal.

In all these circumstances you don't have a choice. You have to leave, either because you're forced to, or you just because you have to for some of the reasons above.

In this situation you should leave as fast as you can. You cannot be in a place that is damaging who you are, so just leave. Seriously. Not having a choice means not having a choice, so leave and take whatever money they owe you and spend 10 days, 15 days or a month pulling yourself together and then start the steps we've outlined in this book. Work through the process.

Not having a choice is different from having one. If you can continue to do what you do for a few months, until you get a new job, and you can work on the steps above while at your position, it's because you have a choice.

If you don't have a choice, do what needs to be done. Just leave and take the extra time you're going to have now, the several hours a day you won't be working, and go through the steps in this process, because then you can increase your chances of getting a new job or getting a new position.

Leaving a bad, damaging job will strengthen your position. When your interviewer asks "why did you leave," you can say, "because my previous company was going against my ethics and I don't comply with that." They will understand you. But if you don't leave and come to an interview and say, "I want to get out because they are doing unethical things," they'll think, "why does she continue to work there then? She must not be very good to put up with that..." So, you'll put yourself in a weak position.

Now, instead of spending time doing things for this company that doesn't deserve you, spend time doing the things that are important for you. If you don't have a choice because you've been fired, well, they're even more important. Do the things we've outlined in this book. Work on them 8, 10, or 15 hours a day. Go deep in all the steps because if you've been fired, you need to be at the top of your game fast. So don't wait, don't procrastinate, work on these things every single day, use the fact that you have the time.

You have time, and time is an opportunity! Now you can apply yourself to a pre-interview project or an open source project or preparing a presentation or going to events and meetups. You might not have money, but you can totally do these at local companies and in your local community. You can do open source. All you need is a computer and the internet. If you don't have a choice, your choice is to do the steps in this program, because they will actually help you get a much better job, much faster.

If you feel you don't have a choice, choose to move now.

References

Some places to get more information and ideas to help you move:

- Code 4 Life - the best career advice for software developers
    - https://code4.life
- All the best advice we could find on how to get a job
    - https://80000hours.org/career-guide/how-to-get-a-job/
- How to Get Any Job You Want (even if you're unqualified)
    - https://medium.com/the-mission/how-to-get-any-job-you-want-even-if-you-re-unqualified-6f49a65f5491
- Pay It Forward With The Five-Minute Favor
    - https://www.forbes.com/sites/kareanderson/2013/07/17/pay-it-forward-with-the-five-minute-favor/#aedcf3c6f5db
- The Basics of Power Networking
    - https://www.linkedin.com/pulse/20130806141819-8244-3-important-things-to-be-mindful-of-as-you-build-your-network/
- 2017 Sources of Hire Report
    - https://www.silkroad.com/blog/2017-sources-of-hire-report/
- How to get employers to give you a chance in an industry where you have no experience
    - https://careers.workopolis.com/advice/the-real-reason-no-one-is-going-to-give-you-a-chance/
- Job Hunting? How to Increase Your Chances of Getting Hired
    - https://www.businessnewsdaily.com/9875-job-hunting-how-to-increase-your-chances-of-getting-hired.html
- Why Asking This 1 Question in a Job Interview Increases the Chances You Get Hired
    - https://www.inc.com/jt-odonnell/managers-say-asking-this-1-question-in-a-job-interview-increases-chances-you-get-hired.html